GET SET! PIANO

Tutor Book 2

Karen Marshall · Heather Hammond

Illustrated by Julia Patton

A & C BLACK MUSIC
AN IMPRINT OF BLOOMSBURY
LONDON NEW DELHI NEW YORK SYDNEY

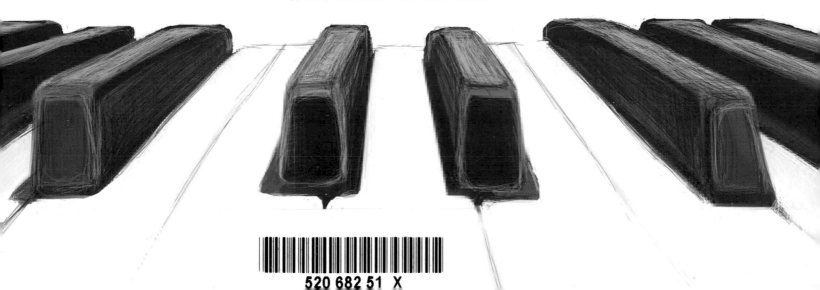

Target practice

- Playing the piano is like doing target practice! If we want to get better, we have to practise regularly and improve over time. Here are some tips:

Tip 1: Get organised!

Practise a little bit each day.

Think about what you're going to practise before you start.

Find a practice time that suits you and stick to it.

Download the Practice Chart printout from the website.

Tip 2: Put your plan into action

- ◯ Check that your sitting and hand positions are correct.
- ◯ Start with piano gym finger exercises or scales and arpeggios to warm up.
- ◯ Practise your pieces hands separately, with the correct fingering, and focus on the tricky bits.
- ◯ Play a new piece to improve your note-reading skills.
- ◯ Do something creative such as composing or performing.

Picture signs for book 2:

- Here are some picture signs that you'll see throughout the book:

 Listen up! games   Find, say and play games

 Rhythm time activities   Website materials

⭐ Challenge pieces trickier but very rewarding pieces

What do you remember from book 1?

- Here are the notes you have learnt so far. Can you find them all on your piano?

- How many crotchet beats is each note worth? Write your answer in the box next to each note.

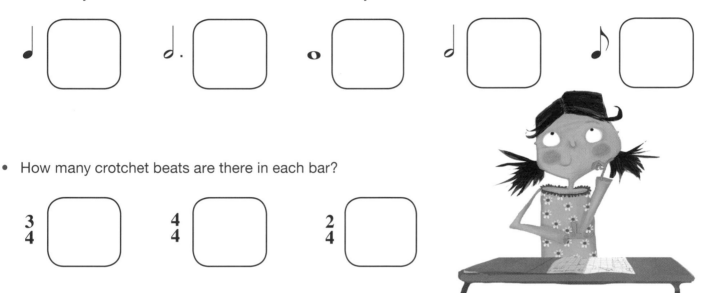

- How many crotchet beats are there in each bar?

$\frac{3}{4}$ ☐ $\frac{4}{4}$ ☐ $\frac{2}{4}$ ☐

- Help the Get set! characters to catch the balloons by drawing a line between each child and the correct answer.

Forte | Repeat sign | Tenuto note | Crescendo | Accent | Staccato note | Flat sign

Getting started

What shall we do with the drunken sailor?

- Can you point to a quaver, a crotchet, a minim and a dotted minim in this piece?

Bright and breezy allegro

traditional, arr. HH

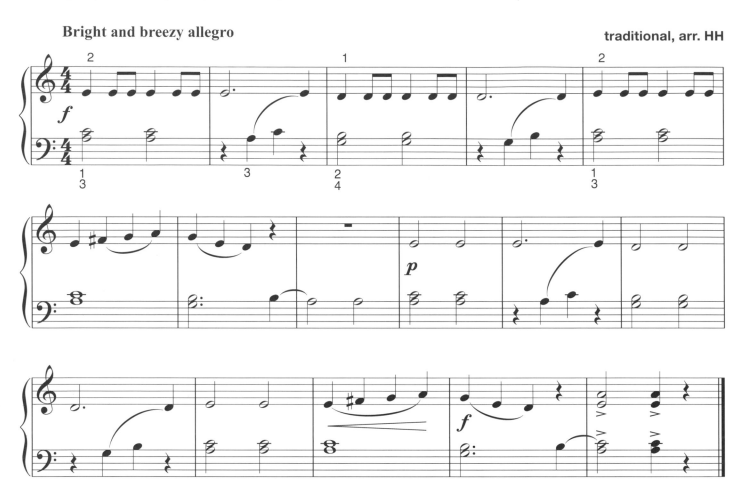

- Try playing the first eight bars of this piece starting on the same notes, higher or lower on the keyboard.

Teacher part:

Get Set! Piano Pieces 2, page 2:

· Michael Finnegan

4

Fun Fiona (for Olivia)

- Can you point to the key signature? Can you point to the notes that need to be flattened and name them?

- How many thirds can you point to in *Fun Fiona*? Your teacher will help you find them.

KM

Dormi chorus

- Can you bounce a ball, one bounce per bar, as your teacher plays *Dormi chorus*?

traditional, arr. KM

Fa   la   la   la   fa   la   la   la   la,

Fa   la   la   la   la   la   fa   la   la   la.

Find, say and play

Get Set! Piano Pieces 2, pages 2-3:

- Imogen's first sketch
- Jumping with Jules

Piano gym

- Try playing these exercises silently on top of the piano keys first.

Get Set! Piano Pieces 2, page 4:
· Over and under together

Squeezing and stretching

KM & HH

KM & HH

Under, over and back to base camp

KM & HH

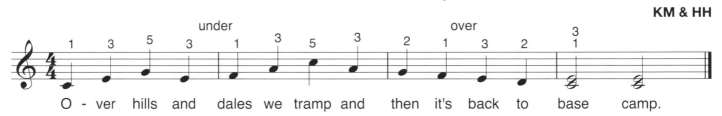

O - ver hills and dales we tramp and then it's back to base camp.

KM & HH

Stretching, squeezing and over we go

words: Lily Stone;
music: HH

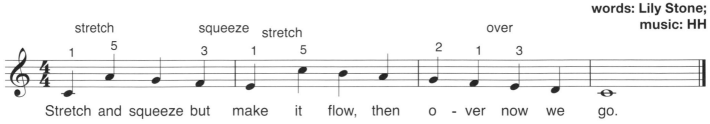

Stretch and squeeze but make it flow, then o - ver now we go.

Try playing these pieces with *forte*, *piano*, *legato* and *staccato* fingers.

New time signature: $\frac{2}{2}$

- $\frac{2}{2}$ means **two minims in a bar**. It can also be written as 𝄵 .

 Listen up!

- Can you clap the pulse as your teacher plays *Cakewalk squeeze*? Make the first clap of each bar slightly louder.

- Your teacher will play you the first four bars of *Cakewalk squeeze* twice. The second time they will change one of the notes. Can you raise your hand when you hear the note that has changed?

Cakewalk squeeze

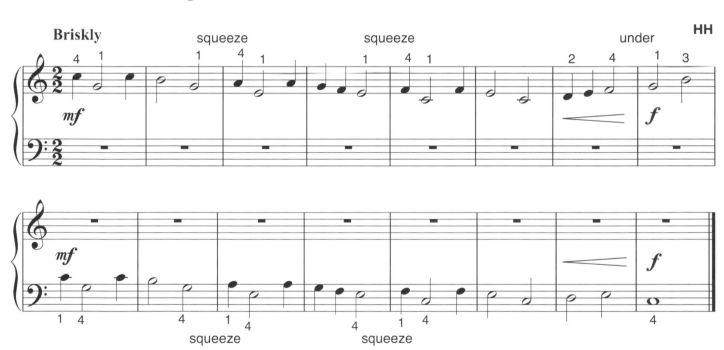

Note to teacher: the pupil part should be played an octave higher when played as a duet.

Teacher part:

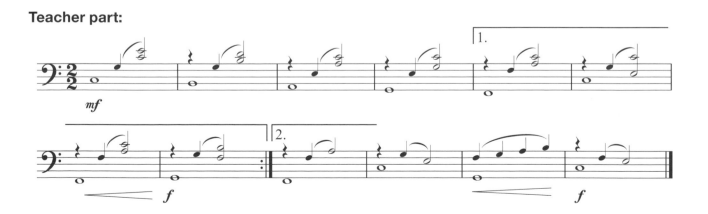

Octaves and intervals

C major scale trail

- Practise this piece hands separately first.

HH

- An **octave** is an interval of **eight notes**. All the scales that you have played up until now have been one octave.

- Now try a two-octave C major scale. Here is the fingering:

Right hand: 1 2 3 1 2 3 4 1 2 3 1 2 3 4 5

Left hand: 5 4 3 2 1 3 2 1 4 3 2 1 3 2 1

- Can you explain to your teacher how the fingering is different from previous scales that you have played?

Intervals a walkin'

- Can you point to the octaves and the *staccato* notes in this piece?

- There is one new interval in this piece called a **sixth**. Can you find it? Your teacher will help you.

Moderato

KM & HH

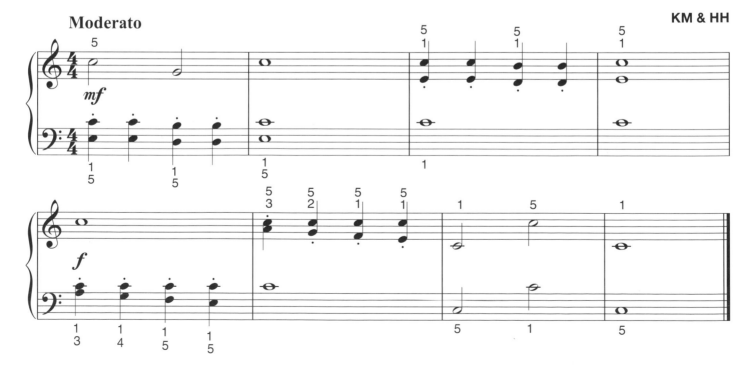

Remember rests?

- **Rests** are signs that tell you to be **silent**.

Quiz

★ How many crotchet beats are these rests worth? Write your answers in the boxes.

Quaver rest

- This is a **quaver rest**: 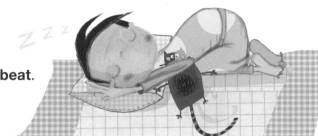 It is worth **half a crotchet beat**.

 Rhythm time

- Your teacher will clap and say the rhyme, then you perform the echo.

- Try counting in quavers to help you with the rhythm.

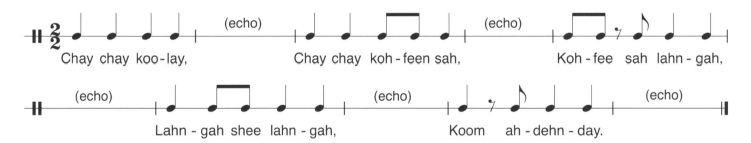

Chay chay koo-lay, (echo) Chay chay koh-feen sah, (echo) Koh-fee sah lahn-gah,

(echo) Lahn-gah shee lahn-gah, (echo) Koom ah-dehn-day. (echo)

Si, si

- Try to play the thirds as smoothly as possible.

Moderato   traditional Congolese, arr. KM

mf Si si si si do la da, Ya ku se ne la du__ ba na ha.

- Can you sing the tune of *Si, si* to your teacher?

New notes: D and E (treble clef)

- Count this rhythm in quavers to help you.

Fourth   line   D   then   top   space   E!

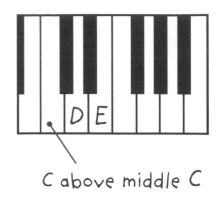

C above middle C

Lavender's blue

- Play this piece **twice**:
  First time: play the 1st-time bars then repeat back to the beginning.
  Second time: miss out the 1st-time bars and go directly to the 2nd-time bars.

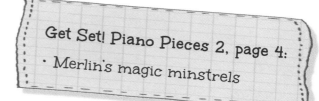

Get Set! Piano Pieces 2, page 4:
· Merlin's magic minstrels

traditional, arr. HH

Happy birthday song

- Practise this piece hands separately first.

KM

We wish you a hap-py birth-day, We wish you a hap-py birth-day. We wish you a hap-py birth-day Na-o-mi you're six.

(Now An-drew you're ten.)

Big jumps and small steps

Kanga jumps

Moderato

KM

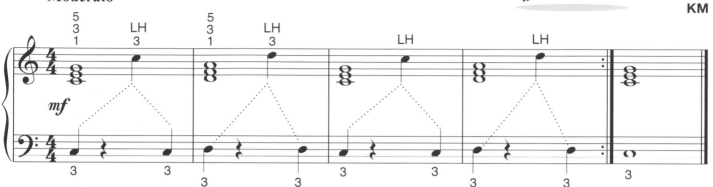

Swimming teacher chant

words: Anna Marshall; music: KM

Moderato

Splash!

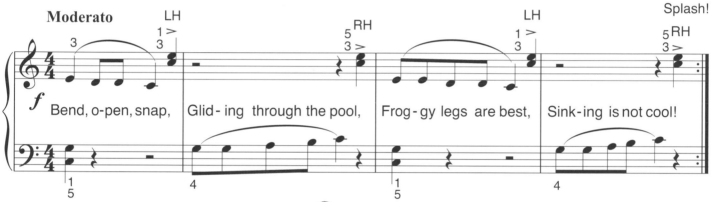

Bend, o-pen, snap, | Glid - ing through the pool, | Frog - gy legs are best, | Sink-ing is not cool!

Tightrope show-off

- **Presto** means very quick (faster than *allegro*).

- Can you point to the *staccato* notes and the *legato* notes in this piece?

Get Set! Piano Pieces 2, page 5:

- Judo James

Presto

HH

mp

mf

New notes: A and B (bass clef)

B   and   A   are com-ing out to   play!

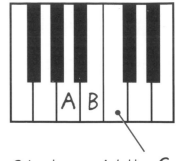

C below middle C

Red Sox rock

- The Red Sox are a baseball team in Boston, Massachusetts, USA.

- Can you point to the repeated patterns in the left-hand part? Try using the left-hand pattern (or **riff**) on the first line as an introduction to the piece.

HH

Funky rock

Get Set! Piano Pieces 2, page 5:
- Over the speed bumps

Can you point to the ties in *Red Sox rock*? Can you explain what a tie is to your teacher?

A harmonic minor scale

Get Set! Piano Pieces 2, page 6:
· Spooks behind the sofa

- Here are the notes for the A harmonic minor scale:

A B C D E F G sharp A

- Can you spot the note that has changed between A natural minor and A harmonic minor?

A harmonic minor scale trail

- The fingering for A harmonic minor is the same as the fingering for A natural minor in both hands.

- Try playing hands separately first.

KM & HH

Listen up!

- Your teacher will play the first four bars of *Feelin' sleepy*. Can you describe the dynamics to them?

Feelin' sleepy (for Harriet C.)

- *Poco* means a little and **adagio** means slow. Therefore **Poco adagio** means a little slow.

KM

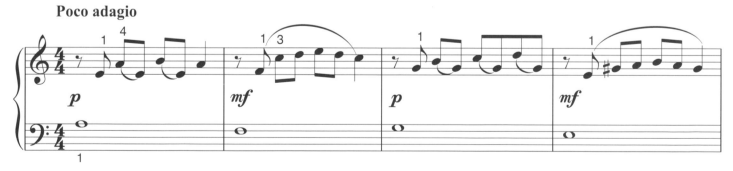

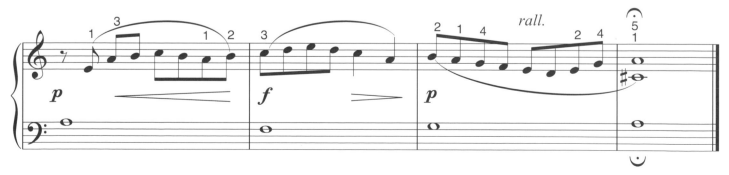

Dotted rhythms

- This is a **dotted crotchet**: ♩. It is worth **three quaver beats**.

- A **dotted minim** is worth **three crotchet beats**.

 Rhythm time

- Can you clap this rhythm with your teacher? Try counting in quavers to help you with the rhythms.

God save our   grac - ious Queen, Long live our   no - ble Queen, God save the Queen.

- The same rhythm can also be written with dotted crotchets instead of tied notes:

God save our   grac - ious Queen, Long live our   no - ble Queen, God save the   Queen.

Alouette

traditional, arr. KM

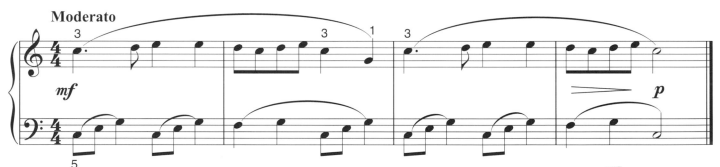

- Can you clap the rhythm, then sing the tune of *Alouette* to your teacher?

> Have you practised your C major, A natural minor and A harmonic minor scales?

Roundabout fun

- ***Cantabile*** means in a singing style.

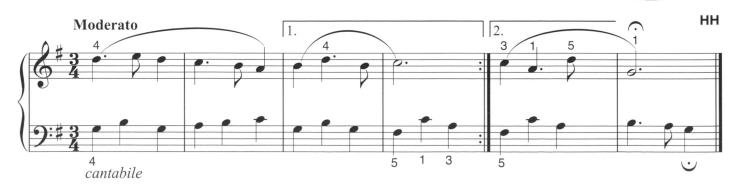

cantabile

HH

New notes: F and G (treble clef)

Top line F just loves to rock, while

G sits on the ve - ry top!

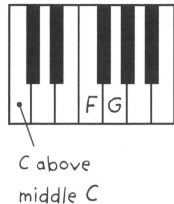

C above
middle C

Simple gifts

- **Rit.** means getting slower/held back.

- Sometimes the left hand also uses the treble clef instead of the bass clef.

traditional, arr. KM

Dancing along

mf

cantabile

f

rit.

Find, say and play

Get Set! Piano Pieces 2,
page 7:

· Dancin' in the rain

15

New key signature: D major

Get Set! Piano Pieces 2,
pages 6 and 8:
- Frère Jacques
- Trumpet tune

- All the Fs and Cs are sharp.

London Bridge is falling down

- **Allegretto** means fairly fast and lively.

Allegretto

traditional, arr. HH

f Lon - don Bridge is | fall - ing down, | Fall - ing down, | fall - ing down.

Lon - don Bridge is | fall - ing down, | My fair | la - dy.

squeeze

Dancin' fingers

Dancin' along

HH

16

New notes: G, F and E (bass clef)

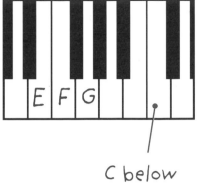

- When you run out of stave lines, the notes sit on extra lines called ledger lines.

Here's a G, F is plain to see, One

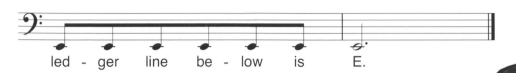

led - ger line be - low is E.

C below middle C

 Listen up!

- Your teacher will play you the first two bars of the right-hand part of *Skateboard skedaddle*. Can you sing it back to them?

Skateboard skedaddle

HH

Teacher part:

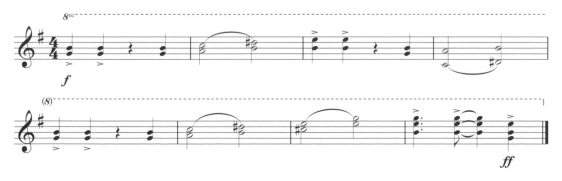

Major and minor scales

Visit the website to download the **Scales Sheet** printout.

Get Set! Piano Pieces 2, page 8:

· Relay runners

Scale trail: G major

KM & HH

Scale trail: D major

KM & HH

Scale trail: D harmonic minor

KM & HH

Scale trail: E harmonic minor

KM & HH

• Practise each scale one octave hands separately, then two octaves hands separately.

New notes: low D and C (bass clef)

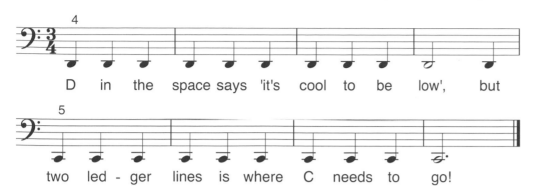

D in the space says 'it's cool to be low', but

two led - ger lines is where C needs to go!

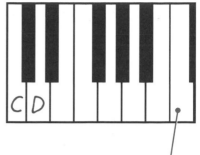

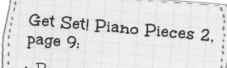

C below middle C

In the hall of the mountain king

Get Set! Piano Pieces 2, page 9:
- Burger boogie

• Can you spot any notes that have two finger numbers in the left hand? Start playing the note with one finger but quickly (whilst still holding the note) swap to the other finger.

Edvard Grieg, arr. HH

F major scale

Get Set! Piano Pieces 2, page 10:
· F major scale trail

- Your teacher will play you the F major scale. Can you work out which note is different from the notes below?

F   G   A   B   C   D   E   F

- Circle the note that is flattened and write in the flat sign next to the note name (the flat sign looks like this: ♭).

F major cluster crunch

- Watch your teacher play F major with their right hand. What was different from the right-hand fingering patterns that you have used previously?

- On the lid of the piano practise:

1   2   3   4   1   2   3   4

- Now try playing this cluster crunch:

F major scale duet 1

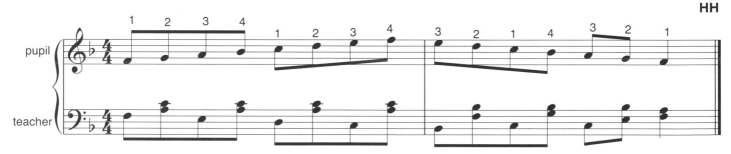

F major scale duet 2

- The left-hand fingering is the same as the fingering for the other scales you have learnt.

Visit the website to download the **Scales Sheet** printout which has more scale duets.

New notes: A, B and C (treble clef)

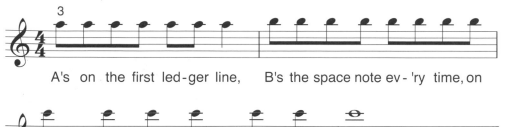

A's on the first led-ger line,   B's the space note ev - 'ry time, on

two   led - ger   lines   we'll   find   C.

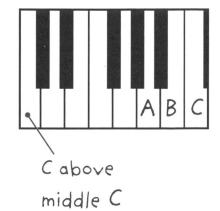

C above
middle C

Boogie on the bus

traditional, arr. KM

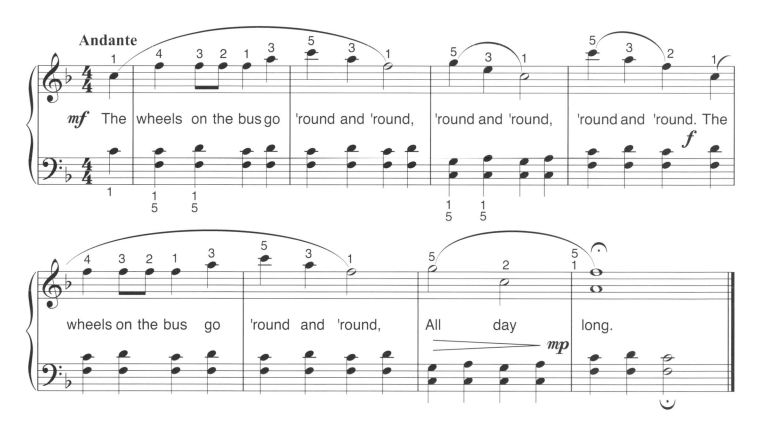

Andante

mf The | wheels on the bus go | 'round and 'round, | 'round and 'round, | 'round and 'round. The *f*

wheels on the bus   go | 'round and 'round, | All   day | long.   *mp*

- Try playing the right-hand part of *Boogie on the bus* an octave lower. Can you sing along at the same time?

Get Set! Piano Pieces 2,
pages 9-10:

· Morning (from Peer Gynt)
· Homework holiday

Both hands in the bass clef

 Listen up!

- Listen to your teacher play *Cadets on parade*. Is it in $\frac{2}{4}$ time or $\frac{3}{4}$ time?

- Can you clap the pulse, making the first beat of the bar stronger?

Cadets on parade

HH

Teacher part:

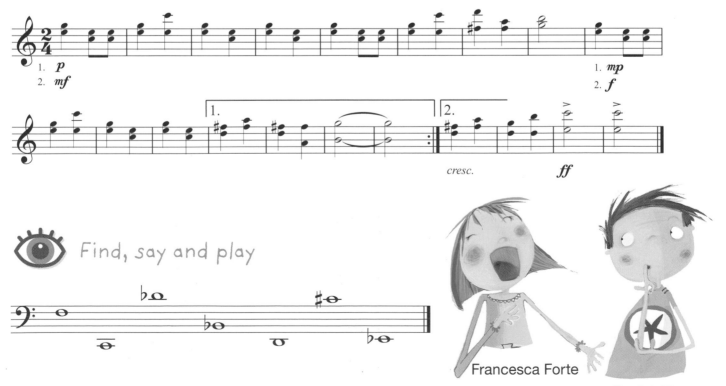

 Find, say and play

Francesca Forte

Patrick Piano

22

Chromatic scales and pieces

- **Chromatic scales** are made up of **semitones**. Start a chromatic scale on any note, then continue playing each neighbouring note.

- Here is a chromatic scale starting on D:

Left hand:

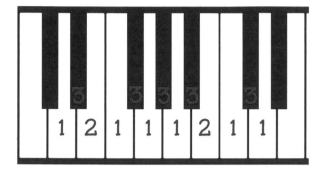

Right hand:

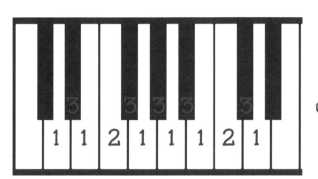

Bring on the clowns

- Can you point to the chromatic scale in the music?

Have you practised your major and minor scales?

HH

Bouncy allegro

mf

ff

Get Set! Piano Pieces 2, page 10:
- Dramatic chromatic

Scales revision

Quiz

★ **Pentascales** are scales with only **five notes**.

★ Write the scale names under each bar, then play the pentascales with firm, strong fingers.

Scale used: C major ....

Scale used: ....

Lazy lullaby

• Can you point to the two scales in *Lazy lullaby*?

KM & HH

24

Primary triads

- Three chords can be used to create an accompaniment to any scale.
  They are called the **primary triads**.

- The primary triads below are in the key of C major. Each one has a special name:

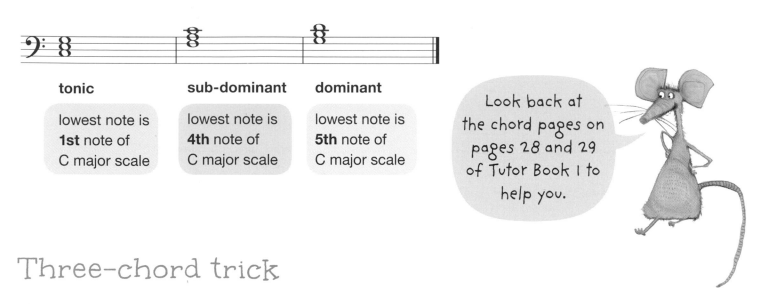

tonic

lowest note is
1st note of
C major scale

sub-dominant

lowest note is
4th note of
C major scale

dominant

lowest note is
5th note of
C major scale

Look back at the chord pages on pages 28 and 29 of Tutor Book I to help you.

Three-chord trick

- Have a go at playing the C major scale using the primary triads as an accompaniment.

- Can you name each primary triad?

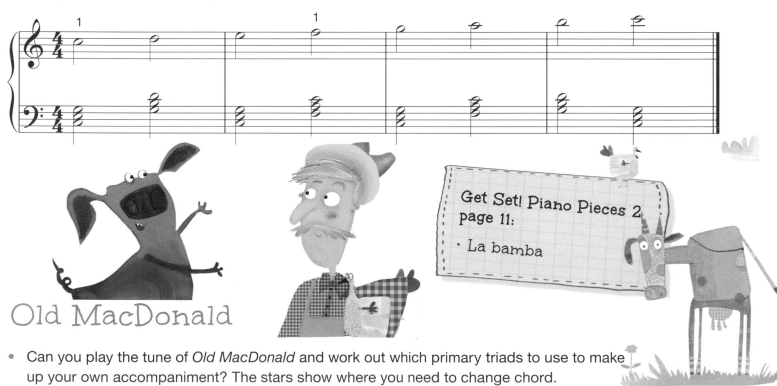

Get Set! Piano Pieces 2 page 11:
- La bamba

Old MacDonald

- Can you play the tune of *Old MacDonald* and work out which primary triads to use to make up your own accompaniment? The stars show where you need to change chord.

traditional

The blues scale

Toot street blues

* **pp** (*pianissimo*) means play very quietly.

HH

Cool moderato (straight quavers)

* Can you tap the pulse as your teacher plays *Toot street blues*?

The blues scale on C

* The **blues scale** is often used by jazz musicians.

* The right hand in *Toot street blues* uses the blues scale. Have a go at playing it:

Get Set! Piano Pieces 2, page 12:
* Your boogie piece
* Move it, groove it!

Your blues scale composition

* Why not compose your own blues piece using the left-hand part from *Toot street blues* and the notes from the blues scale in the right hand in your own order?

* Use the blank score below to write your ideas for the right-hand part. Your teacher will help you with this.

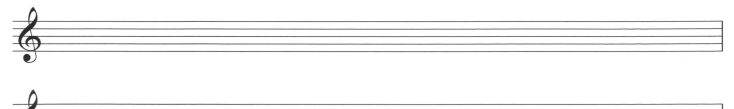

The sustain pedal

- The **pedal** on the **right** is the **sustain pedal**. It makes notes **last longer** by moving the dampers off the strings leaving them to vibrate.

Get Set! Piano Pieces 2, page 13:
- Just in time
- The sorcerer's mirror

- When you press down on the pedal, use the **ball of your foot** and leave your heel on the floor if you are tall enough.

A minor pentascale

- When you see 𝒫𝑒𝑑._____, press down on the sustain pedal until the end of the bracket.

- Using your third finger to play each note, play *A minor pentascale* in *legato* semibreves using the pedal.

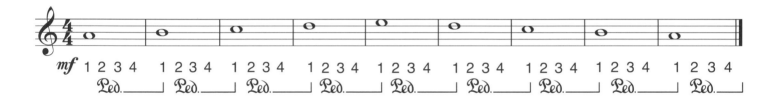

Colourful (for Anna B.)

words: Anna Marshall; music: KM

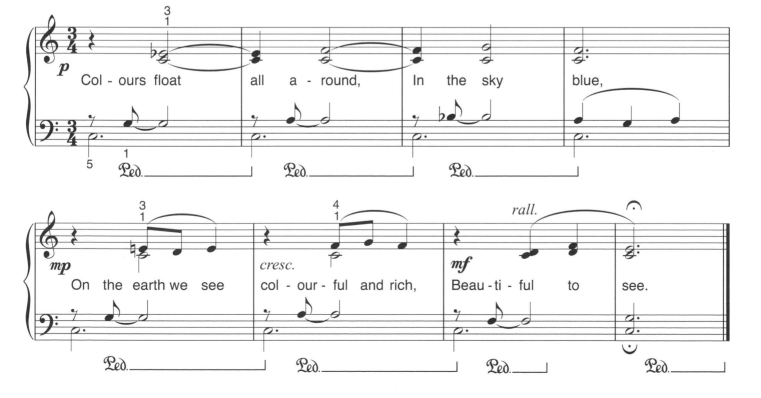

Col - ours float all a - round, In the sky blue,

On the earth we see col - our - ful and rich, Beau - ti - ful to see.

Penny Blue (for P.S.)

- **A tempo** means return to the original speed again.

- **Simile (sim.)** means in the same way, so **ped. sim.** means continue to use the sustain pedal for the whole piece.

Gently flowing

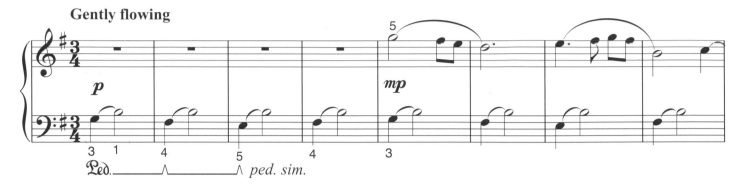

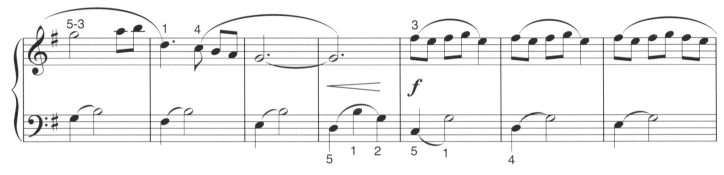

a tempo

The Penny Blue was a British postage stamp that was never actually issued. Instead the Two Pence Blue was issued in 1840.

this note is a high F sharp

Broken chords

- **Broken chords** are chords where the notes are played **separately** instead of at the same time. They come in three positions: **root position**, **first inversion** and **second inversion**.

- Try playing these broken chords, first with the right hand (finger numbers above the notes), then with the left hand (finger numbers below the notes):

Step 1: root position

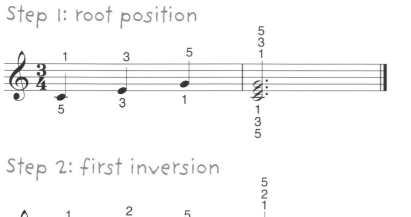

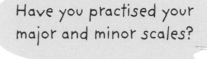

Have you practised your major and minor scales?

Step 2: first inversion

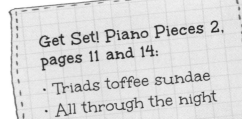

Get Set! Piano Pieces 2, pages 11 and 14:

- Triads toffee sundae
- All through the night

Step 3: second inversion

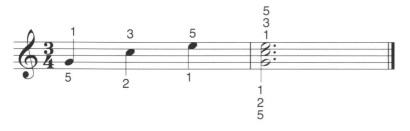

- What do you notice about the order of the notes? Can you tell your teacher?

Broken chord of C major (left and right hands)

Right hand:

Left hand:

- Broken chords can be played in any key. Try working out the broken chords for all the scales you have learnt so far.

New time signature: $\frac{3}{8}$

- $\frac{3}{8}$ means there are **three quavers in each bar**.

Patterns and pedals (for Hugh)

KM

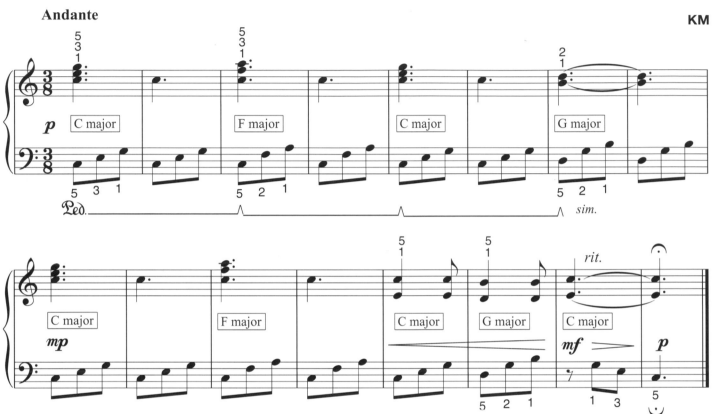

Quiz

★ Answer the questions by completing the stave below.

1. Add a B flat for the key signature.

2. Add the time signature for four crotchets in each bar.

3. Add a C worth one crotchet beat.

4. Add a D worth one crotchet beat.

5. Add a C worth two crotchet beats.

6. Add an A worth one crotchet beat.

7. Add a bar line here.

8. Add an F minim here.

- Do you recognise the tune? Can you work out how it continues and play it to your teacher?

Arpeggios

- An **arpeggio** uses the **first**, **third**, **fifth** and **eighth** notes of a scale.

- Here is the C major arpeggio:

Right hand:

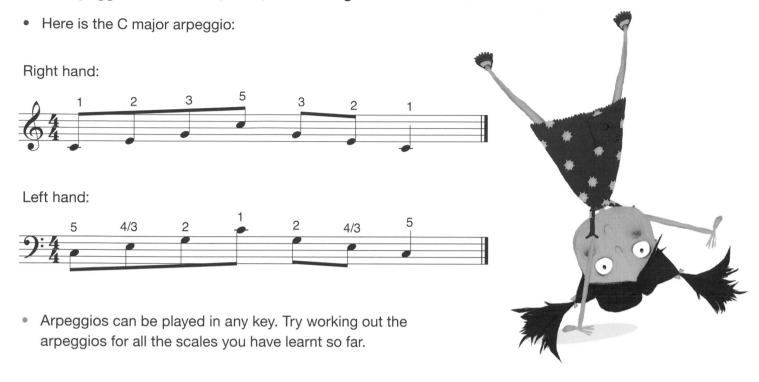

Left hand:

- Arpeggios can be played in any key. Try working out the arpeggios for all the scales you have learnt so far.

Arpeggio slither

- Use a flat hand to play the arpeggio slithers and let your wrist move from side to side:

Left hand:

KM

Right hand:

KM

Find, say and play

31

Broken chord and triad pieces

Skye boat song

- Listen to your teacher play *Skye boat song* to you. Is it *legato* or *staccato*?

traditional, arr. KM

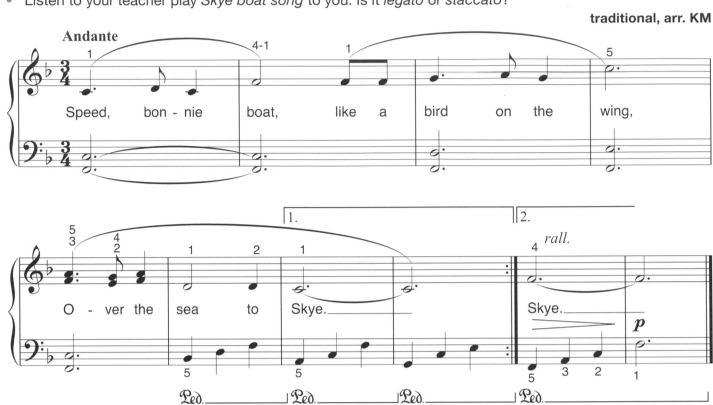

- Can you point to any broken chords and arpeggios in the left-hand part?

Triad virtuoso

- Can you play *Triad virtuoso* from memory and say the chords as you play it?

HH

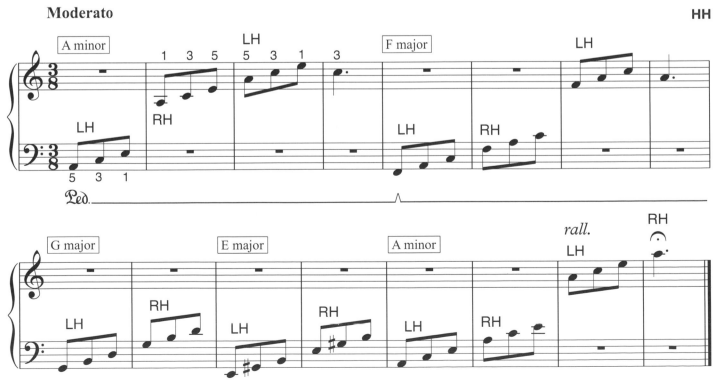

Alberti bass

- An **Alberti bass** is an accompaniment that uses the notes of a triad in this order: lowest, highest, middle, highest.

Get Set! Piano Pieces 2, page 14:

· Balloons floating by

Meet Miss Alberti

traditional, arr. KM

- Composer fact – Mozart used this kind of accompaniment in his Piano Sonata K545.

- Listen to this piece of music on YouTube.com. What can you find out about Mozart and his music?

- What pattern is the right hand playing in this piece?

The lazy dragonfly

- Rock your wrist as if you were turning a door knob as you play the left-hand part.

HH

New time signature: $\frac{6}{8}$

- $\frac{6}{8}$ means **six quavers in a bar**. The quavers are usually grouped in **sets of three**.

Rhythm time

- Can you say the words that go with this rhythm and clap on the accented notes?

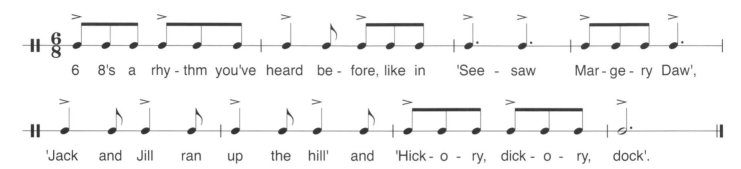

6 8's a rhy-thm you've heard be-fore, like in 'See - saw Mar-ge-ry Daw',

'Jack and Jill ran up the hill' and 'Hick-o-ry, dick-o-ry, dock'.

- Can you make up a tune to go with this rhythm?

Going over the sea

- *Accelerando* means **gradually getting faster**.

- There are two repeat signs in this piece:

  an end repeat: :‖ and

  a start repeat: ‖: which tells you where to go back to.

traditional, arr. KM

Allegretto

f When I was young, I played a drum, Go-ing o-ver the sea. When sea. We're

accelerando

go - ing this way, that way, For-wards and back-wards, O-ver the I-rish Sea.

rit.

Ped.

34

More $\frac{6}{8}$ tunes

Hickory, dickory, dock

- Can you clap the rhythm and say the rhyme?

traditional, arr. KM

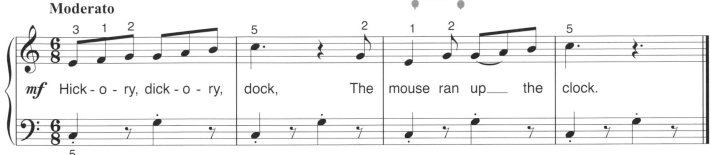

Moderato

mf Hick - o - ry, dick - o - ry, dock, The mouse ran up___ the clock.

- Can you play the rest of the tune?

Get Set! Piano Pieces 2, page 15:
- Martha Murphy's jig

Fiddle-de-dee

- Can you clap the rhythm before you play?

traditional, arr. KM

Jolly moderato

f Fid - dle - de - dee, fid - dle - de - dee, The fly has mar - ried the bum - ble bee.

this note is a high E

Ladybird

traditional, arr. KM

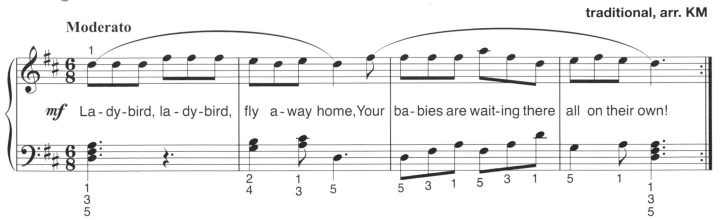

Moderato

mf La - dy-bird, la - dy-bird, fly a - way home, Your ba - bies are wait-ing there all on their own!

Phrasing

- A **phrase** is a **musical sentence**. Phrases have large curved lines above them, like umbrellas.

- Between each phrase there is a **very short silence** (like taking a breath in a song).

Kum ba ya

- Listen to your teacher play the tune of *Kum ba ya*. Is the last note of this piece higher, lower or the same as the first note?

traditional, arr. KM

Granny Annie's tango

HH

Acciaccaturas

Get Set! Piano Pieces 2, page 16:
· Keel row

- An **acciaccatura** (pronounced *aki-aka-chura*) is a very short note played just before another note. It is shown by a little note with a line through it:

Eve's fiddle (for Eve)

- To play the *acciaccatura* notes, put the two notes down at the same time then quickly come off the *acciaccatura*, leaving the other note to sound.

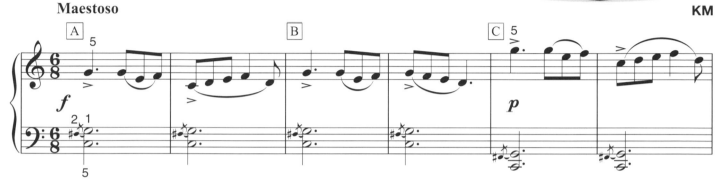

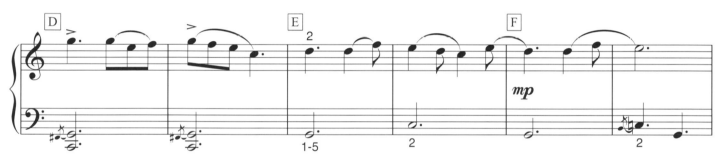

Quiz

★ Can you play the sections of *Eve's fiddle* in this order?   F   D   H   A   C   G   E   B

★ Make up your own musical puzzle by choosing your own order in which to play the various sections of *Eve's fiddle*? Write the order below, then try playing it.

....

Syncopation

Get Set! Piano Pieces 2, page 16:
· Zoom zone

- **Syncopation** is when notes are played just **before** or **after** the main beat, where you don't expect them.

Al - a - bam - a gals, won't you come out to- night? Come out to - night, come out to - night?

- Can you make up a tune for this syncopated rhythm?

Raspberry ripple rumba

- *Con moto* means **with movement**.

- Remember to keep your right wrist relaxed as it rocks gently from side to side.

- Is the left hand or the right hand syncopated?

Quiz

- What do these words mean?

  allegretto ....

  andante ....

  allegro ....

  con moto ....

  moderato ....

  largo ....

Swung quavers

- Search for 'Hey, Mr Miller' on YouTube.com and listen to the song. Can you describe to your teacher how the quavers sound different to the ones you have played before?

- The quavers in *Hey, Mr Miller* are **swung**. This means that we make the first quaver slightly longer than the second quaver to give the music a jazzy feel.

Get Set! Piano Pieces 2, page 17:

- Cowboy MacDonald

Hey, Mr Miller

David Machell, arr. HH

Con moto, swung quavers

mf Hey, Mis-ter Mil-ler, What a swing that you bring to the band,

Hey, Mis-ter Mil-ler, What a swing that you bring to the band, *p* With your

trom-bone and your sax-o-phone, You can hear it all through the land, *f* With your

trom-bone and your sax-o-phone, You can hear it all through the land.

- The last part of the song hasn't been included in the music above. Can you spot it in the YouTube version? It starts with a C major arpeggio.

- With your teacher's help can you work out the last part of the song by using your ears and experimenting?

Semiquavers

- This is a **semiquaver**: ♪

- There are **four** semiquavers in a **crotchet beat**.

 Rhythm time

Bub-ble gum, bub-ble gum, chew and blow,   Bub-ble gum, bub-ble gum, scrape it off your toe.

Bub-ble gum, bub-ble gum, tastes ve - ry sweet,   Get that bub-ble gum off your feet!

- Can you make up a tune for this rhythm?

 Listen up!

- Your teacher will play you two bars from *The rhythm juggle* twice. The second time they will change one rhythm. Raise your hand when you hear the change.

The rhythm juggle

- Make sure that you play *The rhythm juggle* slowly first. Your teacher could play the left hand for you to begin with.

KM & HH

Moderato

mf

 Rhythm time

- Can you fit any of these words to the rhythms in *The rhythm juggle*?

1) Caterpillar   2) Strawberry   3) Lemonade

Pirates ahoy!

- This sign: 8^{va-} asks you to play **an octave higher than the notes are written**.

Get Set! Piano Pieces 2, pages 17–19:
- Musette in D
- Mr Bartok and Miss Brown trio

HH

Daffodil

C. Gurlitt

this note is a low G

Piano gym

Fingers play their part

Adagio

KM

Rocking wrist toccata

KM

Five-finger workout

based on Carl Czerny's 101 exercises, op. 26, no. 41, arr. KM

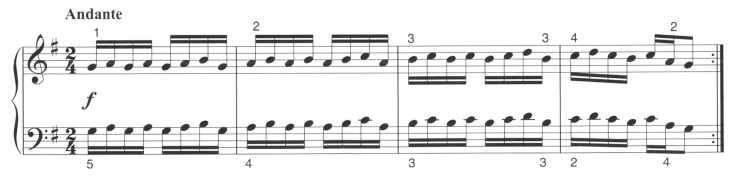

Loose wrist

KM

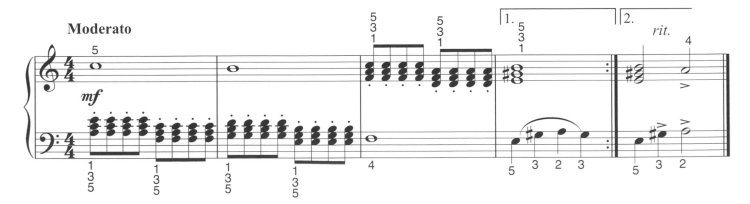

New time signatures: $\frac{5}{4}$ and $\frac{5}{8}$

- Most time signatures can usually be divided into either **two-time** or **three-time**. This means that they either have **two or three beats in each bar**.

- There are some more unusual time signatures that cannot be divided up in this way, for example $\frac{5}{4}$ or $\frac{5}{8}$.

Windmills

- Can you point to where the time signature changes?

HH

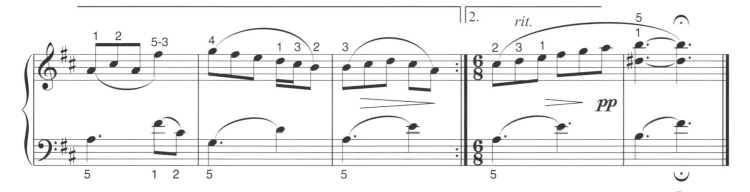

Dinosaurs' dance

- Notes with dots inside a slur mean that you play semi-*staccato* (slightly separated).

Get Set! Piano Pieces 2, page 21:
- Telling silly stories

HH

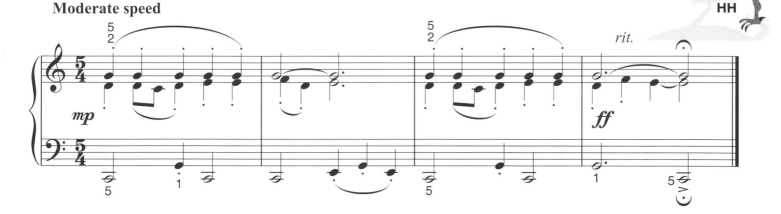

Triplets

Get Set! Piano Pieces 2, page 22:

- This old man
- Meet the triplets

- A **triplet** is where **three notes** are played **in the space of one beat**.

 are played in the time of 

 are played in the time of 

Rhythm time

Ne - ver too sharp, ne - ver too sweet, Black-ber - ry jam is so love - ly to eat!

- Can you make up a tune to go with this rhythm?

Gavotte

W. Duncombe

Gracefully

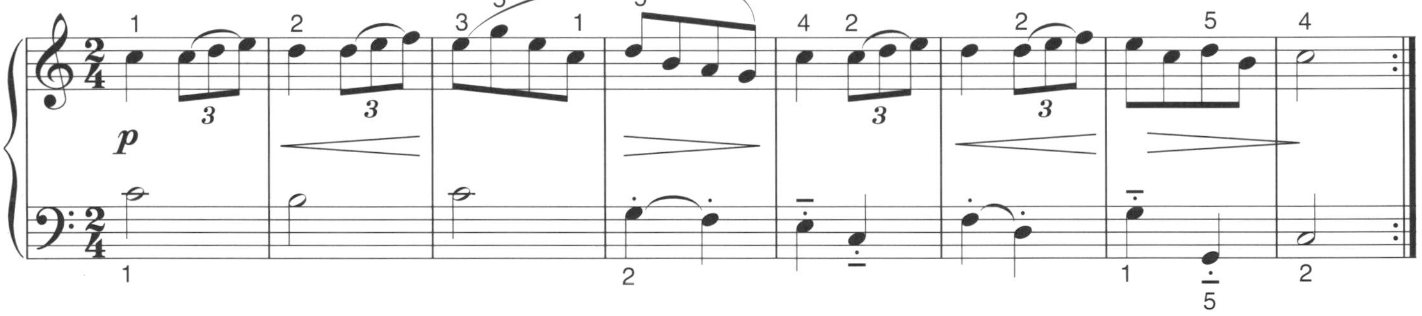

Amazing grace

traditional, arr. HH

Andante

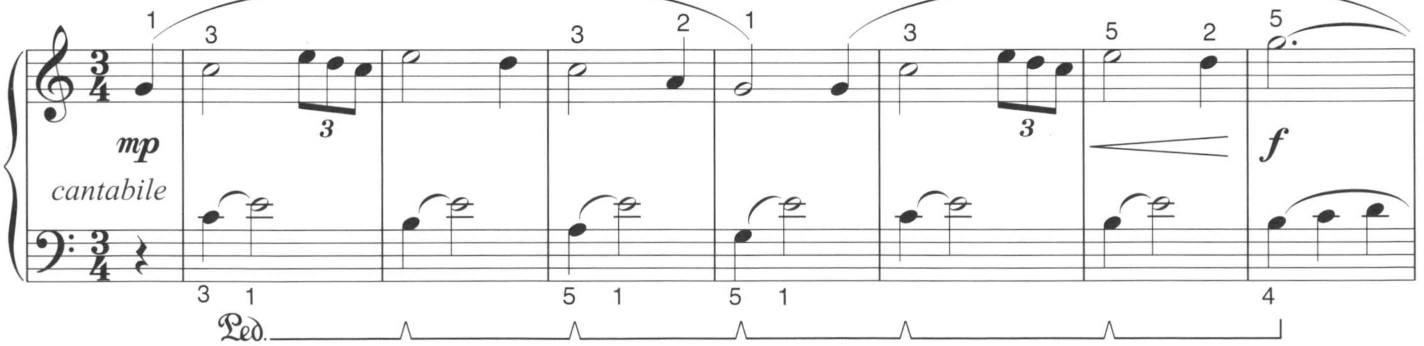

mp
cantabile
f

mf
mp
p

A new dotted rhythm

Get Set! Piano Pieces 2, page 23:
- Brand new puppy

- A **dotted quaver** ♪. is worth **three semiquavers**.

Bele mama (Call mama)

Moderato

traditional

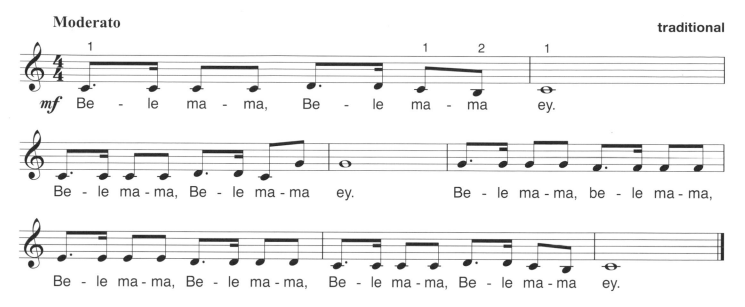

mf Be - le ma - ma, Be - le ma - ma ey.

Be - le ma - ma, Be - le ma - ma ey. Be - le ma - ma, be - le ma - ma,

Be - le ma - ma, Be - le ma - ma, Be - le ma - ma, Be - le ma - ma ey.

- Can you make up a left-hand part for *Bele mama* using the tonic triads from C major, F major and G major?

Molly's minuet (for Molly) ⭐

KM

Maestoso

Concert pieces 1

Gavotta in C

- A *gavotta* is a **French folk dance**.

James Hook

Dancing along

Quiz for *Gavotta in C*

★ How many minim beats are there in each bar? ....

★ What does this sign mean? ⟋ ....

★ What does this sign ask you to do? > ....

★ What is the Italian name for this sign? *mf* ....

★ What does this sign ask you to do? :‖ ....

46

Concert pieces 2

Monty's secret mission

- *sfz* is an abbreviation for the word ***sforzando***
  meaning **with force** (like a strong accent).

Get Set! Piano Pieces 2,
pages 20 and 24:
- Sneaky midnight cat
- Pachelbel goes pop

With determination

HH

this note is a low A

Concert pieces 3

 Listen up!

- Your teacher will play you the last line of the right-hand part of *The Entertainer*, missing out the last note. Can you sing it?

The Entertainer

Scott Joplin, arr. HH

Keep it steady, don't rush!

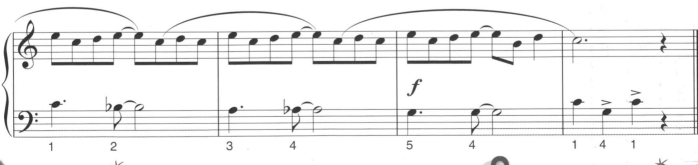

Congratulations!

You have now finished *Get Set! Piano Tutor Book 2*. Ask your teacher or parent to download and print out your certificate from the Get Set! website: **www.bloomsbury.com/getsetpianotutor2**